LAUGH
—OUT—
LOUD

POCKET

Doodles

FOR GIRLS

Books by Rob Elliott

Laugh-Out-Loud Jokes for Kids
More Laugh-Out-Loud Jokes for Kids
Laugh-Out-Loud Animal Jokes for Kids
Laugh-Out-Loud Knock-Knock Jokes for Kids
Big Book of Laugh-Out-Loud Jokes for Kids
Laugh-Out-Loud Doodles for Kids
Laugh-Out-Loud Pocket Doodles for Girls
Laugh-Out-Loud Pocket Doodles for Boys

LAUGH
—OUT—
LOUD

Doodles

FOR GIRLS

ROB ELLIOTT

ILLUSTRATED BY JONNY HAWKINS

Revell

a division of Baker Publishing Group
Grand Rapids, Michigan

Text © 2015 by Rob Elliott
Illustrations © 2015 by Jonny Hawkins

Published by Revell
a division of Baker Publishing Group
P.O. Box 6287, Grand Rapids, MI 49516-6287
www.revellbooks.com

Printed in the United States of America

ISBN 978-0-8007-2237-1

15 16 17 18 19 20 21   7 6 5 4 3 2 1

THE LAUGH-OUT-LOUD HUMOR CODE
by Rob Elliott

1. Don't make jokes at other people's expense.

2. Keep it clean.

3. Laughter is great medicine, so find something to laugh at every day.

NOT TO BE TAKEN SERIOUSLY

4. Tell your favorite jokes to as many people as you can to brighten up their days, too!

5. Body noise and body fluid jokes are best.

HICCUP

MY HUMOR CODE

1.

2.

3.

4.

5.

Write and doodle your own humor code.

Picture yourself telling your favorite joke.
Doodle it . . . and draw your crowd too!

Q: WHAT KIND OF FLOWERS ARE GREAT FRIENDS?

A: ROSEBUDS.

Doodle her friend and what they do
to grow their friendship.

Q: WHY DID THE LADY WEAR A HELMET EVERY TIME SHE ATE?

A: SHE WAS ON A CRASH DIET!

Doodle the lady and what she is eating.

Q: WHAT DO YOU CALL A FAIRY THAT DOESN'T TAKE A BATH?

A: STINKERBELL.

Doodle her in all of her pixie dust . . . cough, cough!

Q: WHAT DO YOU CALL THE STORY OF THE THREE LITTLE PIGS?

A: A PIGTAIL.

Doodle the other two pigs and their houses.

Q: WHY DID THE CAT AND HER KITTENS
CLEAN UP THEIR MESS?

A: THEY DIDN'T WANT TO LITTER.

Doodle the mama cat and more
kittens. Doodle more cleanup.

Q: WHAT DID THE TOOTH FAIRY USE
   TO FIX HER WAND?

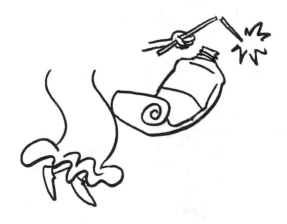

A: TOOTHPASTE.

Doodle the rest of the fairy. How
is she fixing the wand?

Q: WHO HELPED THE MONSTER
   GO TO THE BALL?

A: ITS SCARY GODMOTHER.

Doodle the hideous fairy and what
the monster becomes.

Q: WHAT KIND OF MAKEUP DO PIRATE
   GIRLS WEAR?

A: SHIP GLOSS.

Finish the pirate girl, and arrgh . . . draw another.

Q: WHY DID THE QUEEN GO TO THE DENTIST?

A: TO GET CROWNS ON HER TEETH.

Doodle the royal dentist and what he is doing to the royal teeth.

Q: WHAT DO YOU GET WHEN YOU CROSS A FLOWER, A CAR, AND THE USA?

A: A PINK CAR NATION.

Who's driving? Doodle a flower on the car. Color it pink!

Q: WHAT DID THE BRIDE SAY WHEN SHE DROPPED HER BOUQUET?

A: "WHOOPSY-DAISIES."

Doodle her downed bouquet and her groom.

KNOCK KNOCK.
   WHO'S THERE?
LITTLE OLD LADY.
   LITTLE OLD LADY WHO?
I DIDN'T KNOW YOU COULD YODEL!

Doodle a lady yodeling.

A: IT HAD A VIRUS.

Doodle the sneezy computer with a bug.

Q: WHAT PLAYS MUSIC ON YOUR HEAD?

A: A HEADBAND.

Doodle this noted musical group.

Q: HOW DOES MOSES MAKE HIS TEA?

A: HEBREWS IT.

Doodle the way he makes his tea
and draw the rest of his body.

Q: WHAT DID THE LIPSTICK SAY TO THE EYE SHADOW?

A: "WE SHOULD STOP FIGHTING AND MAKEUP!"

Doodle the eye shadow and other makeup.

Q: WHERE DO BEES GO WHEN THEY GET MARRIED?

A: ON THEIR HONEYMOON.

Doodle the groom. Where are they buzzing off to?

A: MICE KRISPIES.

Decorate the box. What's in the bowl?

Q: WHY DID THE BOAT
GO TO THE MALL?

A: SHE WAS LOOKING FOR A SAIL.

Hoist her find! And decorate it!

Q: WHY COULDN'T THE SKUNK
   GO SHOPPING?

A: SHE DIDN'T HAVE A SCENT IN HER WALLET.

Doodle her purse, its contents, and the rest of her.

Q: WHAT'S A SWAN'S FAVORITE
CHRISTMAS CAROL?

A: DUCK THE HALLS.

Doodle the rest of the swan and
her holiday decorations!

Q. WHAT DO YOU CALL A POLAR BEAR IN HAWAII?

A: LOST!

Doodle a volcano, palm trees, and
other Hawaiian background.

A: SHE REALLY KNEADED THE DOUGH!

We really "knead" you to finish this joke! What is
she making? Doodle her tools, dishes, and table.

Q: HOW DID THE PIG WRITE A LETTER?

A: WITH A PIGPEN.

Doodle the pig's head. What is she thinking?

Q: WHY DID THE CHICKEN GO TO BED?

A: SHE WAS EGGS-HAUSTED!

Doodle the rest of the bed. Where are her eggs?

Q: WHY DID THE CAT GO TO THE BEAUTY SALON?

A: IT NEEDED A PET-ICURE.

Where is the beautician? Give kitty a fur do!

A: SOCK PUPPIES.

Doodle others in the litter.

Q: WHAT IS THE DIFFERENCE BETWEEN A CAT AND A FROG?

A: A CAT HAS NINE LIVES AND A FROG CROAKS EVERY DAY.

Finish the friends and their funny faces.

Q: WHAT DO BEARS WEAR
   IN THEIR HAIR?

A: BEARRETTES.

Doodle the bearrettes . . . make 'em fancy!

Q: WHAT KIND OF FISH COMES OUT AT NIGHT?

A: A STARFISH.

You are so bright! Now doodle the joke!

Q: WHY WAS THE BIRD ALWAYS CRYING?

A: IT WAS A BLUEBIRD.

What's making the bird so blue? Gummy worms?

Q: WHY CAN'T YOU WIN AN ARGUMENT
   WITH A PENCIL?

A: IT'S ALWAYS WRITE.

Doodle the rest of the face, the head, and the neck

Q: WHAT DID THE BABY CORN SAY
   TO THE MOMMY CORN?

A: "WHERE IS POPCORN?"

Put a face on the ear of corn. Draw Dad in back.

Q: WHAT DID THE CELL PHONE SAY TO THE LANDLINE?

A: "HI, GRANDMA!"

Finish the line. Add some birdies line dancing.

Q: WHAT KIND OF KEYS ARE EASY
   TO SWALLOW?

A: COOKIES.

Who will eat these? Doodle them!

Q: WHAT DO YOU GET WHEN YOU CROSS A HORSE WITH A PENCIL?

A: HORSEBACK WRITING.

Doodle the horse's letter . . . and a stable background.

Q: WHY DID THE HORSE GO TO THE PSYCHIATRIST?

A: IT WAS FEELING UN-STABLE.

Where's the psychiatrist? Draw his certificate on the wall.

Q: WHY DID THE SHOE FALL IN LOVE
   WITH THE BOOT?

A: BECAUSE THEY WERE SOLE MATES.

Doodle the boot and hearts above them. Aww.

A: BEAR-FOOT.

Doodle the un-fur-gettable feet!

Q: WHY WAS THE TEACHER WEARING SUNGLASSES INSIDE?

A: BECAUSE SHE HAD SUCH BRIGHT STUDENTS!

Doodle some of those bright kids. Make 'em shine!

Q: WHY DID THE GIRL EAT HER HOMEWORK?

A: THE TEACHER SAID IT WOULD BE A PIECE OF CAKE.

Fill in the thought balloon with gloriously decorated cake!

Q: WHY DID THE BOOK JOIN THE POLICE FORCE?

POLICE

A: IT WANTED TO GO UNDERCOVER.

Doodle the book and tell its story.

Q: WHY DID THE SONG GET AN A+
ON ITS TEST?

A: BECAUSE IT TOOK A LOT OF NOTES.

Doodle the classroom around the song.

KNOCK KNOCK.
  WHO'S THERE?
ANNETTE.
  ANNETTE WHO?
YOU NEED ANNETTE TO PLAY
  VOLLEYBALL.

Doodle the door answerer wrapped in a net.

Q: WHAT IS THE CLEANEST STATE?

A: WASHINGTON.

Doodle a bucket and a mop. Why is she
washing the mountain? Show all that dirt!

Q: WHAT KIND OF SHOES DO BAKERS WEAR?

A: LOAF-ERS.

Doodle the rest of the baker and more homemade clothes. Mmm.

Q: WHAT DID THE HAMBURGER NAME ITS FIRST CHILD?

A: PATTY.

Doodle a cute little baby burger.

Q: WHY DID THE ELEPHANTS TAKE UP
THE LEAST AMOUNT OF ROOM
ON NOAH'S ARK?

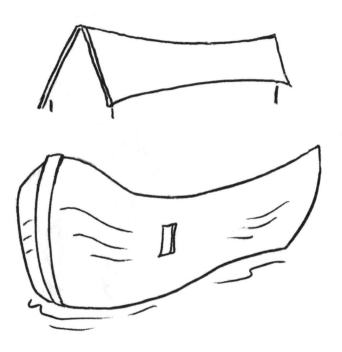

A: BECAUSE THEY KEPT EVERYTHING IN THEIR TRUNKS.

Fill up the boat with animals two by
two. Where are the elephants?

Q: WHY WERE THE LAMB AND GOAT
   SUCH GOOD FRIENDS?

A: BECAUSE THEY HAD A VERY CLOSE RELATION-SHEEP.

Draw the lamb with her BFF. Baaaa-eautiful!

Q: HOW DO YOU KNOW WHEN IT'S BEEN RAINING CATS AND DOGS?

A: WHEN YOU STEP IN A POODLE.

Who is stepping? Doodle other raining cats and dogs.

Q: WHAT DO YOU CALL KIDS WHO PLAY OUTSIDE IN THE SNOW?

A: CHILLED-REN.

Chill out and doodle another cold child
. . . this one building a snowman.

Q: HOW DO YOU MAKE FRIENDS WITH EVERYONE AT SCHOOL?

A: YOU BECOME A PRINCI-PAL.

Doodle a student or two having a
nice visit with the man.

Q: WHAT HAPPENS TO STRAWBERRIES
WHEN THEY ARE SAD?

A: THEY BECOME BLUEBERRIES.

Doodle the sad joke and add a surprise fruit.

Q: WHAT KIND OF CATS LIKE TO PLAY
   IN THE OCEAN?

A: SEA LIONS.

Doodle the rest of him playing . . . and
playing! Does he have friends nearby?

A: "BONE VOYAGE!"

Finish the pooch and doodle oodles of other poodles.

A: BECAUSE IT WAS DRAINED.

Rub-a-dub-dub, fill up the tub. Doodle shampoo and soap and duckies.

Q: WHAT DID THE DOG SAY
    TO ITS OWNER?

A: "I WOOF YOU!"

Where is the owner? Is it you?

Q: WHAT DID THE GIRL SAY WHEN SHE THREW A SLUG ACROSS THE ROOM?

A: "MY, HOW SLIME FLIES!"

Doodle a flying slug and something it's about to hit.

Q: WHAT DID THE WORM SAY TO HER
DAUGHTER WHEN SHE CAME HOME
LATE?

A: "WHERE ON <u>EARTH</u> HAVE YOU BEEN?"

Doodle the upset parent and the rest of the joke.

Q: WHAT DO YOU GET WHEN YOU CROSS BAMBI WITH AN UMBRELLA?

A: A RAIN-DEER.

Decorate our deer one's umbrella.

Q: WHY DID THE GIRL STOP USING
   THE PENCIL?

A: IT WAS POINTLESS.

Draw what broke her lead. Draw her drawing.

Q: WHAT IS A COW'S FAVORITE PAINTING?

A: THE MOO-NA LISA.

Doodle this masterpiece.

Q: WHY DID THE POLICE ARREST
   THE CHICKEN?

A: THEY SUSPECTED FOWL PLAY.

Finish the big chicken.

Q: WHAT DID THE COMPOSER SAY AFTER THE SYMPHONY?

A: "I'LL BE BACH."

Finish this fair and noted composer.

Q: WHAT DO FROGS EAT ON REALLY HOT DAYS?

A: HOP-SICLES.

Finish the refreshed froggies as they lick and hop.

A: ELK-ASELTZER.

Finish off the poor old deer.

Q: WHY DID THE BIRD GO TO
   THE HOSPITAL?

A: TO GET SOME MEDICAL TWEETMENT.

Draw the awaiting doctor and nurse.

Q: WHY ARE SHEEP SO GULLIBLE?

A: BECAUSE IT'S EASY TO PULL
THE WOOL OVER THEIR EYES.

Who is pulling the wool over this sheepish
one? Draw another sheep too.

Q: WHY COULDN'T ALL THE KING'S HORSES AND ALL THE KING'S MEN PUT HUMPTY DUMPTY TOGETHER AGAIN?

A: BECAUSE THEY WERE EGGS-HAUSTED!

Where's Humpty Dumpty? Scrambled?
Draw one of the king's men.

A: "THE BUCK STOPS HERE!"

Doodle the corrected fawn . . . and
a buck off in the distance.

Q: WHAT IS SMARTER THAN
   A TALKING CAT?

A: A SPELLING BEE.

Bee smart and finish the speller. Bees waiting?

A: SHE WANTED TO GET THE SCOOP!

What is her question? Who is she interviewing? Decorate the parlor.

Q: WHY SHOULD YOU ALWAYS BE NICE
   TO A HORSE?

A: BECAUSE YOU SHOULD LOVE
   YOUR NEIGH-BOR AS YOURSELF.

Draw yourself as a horse trainer.
What is horsie saying?

Q: WHAT DID THE GIRL OYSTER SAY TO THE BOY OYSTER?

A: "YOU ALWAYS CLAM UP WHEN I TRY TO TALK TO YOU!"

Draw the boy oyster and other deep-sea life.

Q: WHAT DO SNOWMEN LIKE BEST AT SCHOOL?

A: SNOW AND TELL.

What is he showing and saying?

Q: WHAT DO YOU GET FROM GRUMPY COWS?

A: SOUR MILK.

What is she carrying? Doodle it!

Q: WHY DID THE PONY WAKE UP
   IN THE MIDDLE OF THE NIGHT?

A: BECAUSE SHE HAD A NIGHT-MARE!

Where's the rest of her bed? And
what's going through her head?

Q: HOW DO YOU KNOW THAT EATING CARROTS IS GOOD FOR YOUR EYES?

A: WELL, HAVE YOU EVER SEEN A RABBIT WITH GLASSES?

Doodle the rabbits who nibbled these carrots. Who's wearing glasses?

Q: WHAT KIND OF BEAR STAYS OUT IN THE RAIN?

A: A DRIZZLY BEAR.

Doodle the raindrops of all shapes and sizes.

Q: WHY DID THE BUNNY
   GO TO THE HOSPITAL?

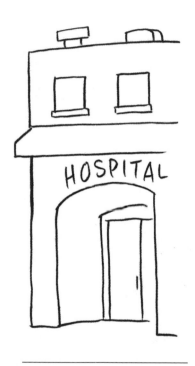

A: IT NEEDED A HOP-ERATION.

Where's the bunny and her mommy? What's hurting?

Q: WHO HELPS PIGS FALL IN LOVE?

A: CU-PIG.

Doodle the hog and the swine that swooned!

Q: WHEN IS A COW HAPPY, THEN SAD, AND THEN ANGRY?

A: WHEN IT'S MOO-DY.

Draw the moo-ving and moo-dy faces.

Q: WHAT DO DEER KEEP
   THEIR LUNCHES IN?

A: BUCK-ETS.

Finish our deer friend. Draw the forest behind him.

Q: WHAT IS A DUCK'S FAVORITE SNACK?

A: CHEESE AND QUACKERS.

Finish the joke! Draw something that will quack you up!

Q: WHY DID THE CHICKENS GET
IN TROUBLE AT SCHOOL?

A: THEY WERE USING FOWL LANGUAGE.

Where's the teacher? Fill in the classroom.

A: A DANDY-LION.

Doodle the happy head and the main mane.

Q: WHY DID THE TURKEY HAVE
A TUMMY ACHE?

A: IT GOBBLED UP ITS FOOD TOO FAST.

Draw the big feathery plumage behind the turkey.

Q: WHAT DO SKUNKS LIKE TO EAT
WHEN THEY'RE HUNGRY?

A: PEANUT BUTTER AND SMELLY SANDWICHES.

Draw the big, poofy tail with the
white stripe down the middle.

Q: WHAT DO YOU GET WHEN YOU PUT GLASSES ON A PONY?

A: A SEE HORSE.

Put pony's glasses on. Design other funny specs in the display case.

Q: WHAT DO FISH LIKE TO SING DURING THE HOLIDAYS?

A: CHRISTMAS CORALS.

Doodle a couple more fishy coralers.
And to whom are they singing?

Q: WHAT DO YOU GET WHEN THERE'S A BUNCH OF GIRAFFES ON THE HIGHWAY?

A: A GIRAFFE-IC JAM.

Doodle more giraffes in their vehicles.

Q: WHAT DO YOU CALL A GREASY BUG?

A: A BUTTER-FLY.

Doodle a butter body with wide eyes and a shiny smile.

TONGUE TWISTER: COLORING WITH CRAYONS CAN CAUSE CRAMPING.

Doodle her crayon works of art. Draw a huge monster crayon in the background.

Q: WHERE DO BUGS GO TO DO THEIR SHOPPING?

A: THE FLEA MARKET.

We bet you're itching to doodle this joke!

A: POUND CAKE!

Doodle the doggone joke!

Q: HOW DO YOU KNOW IF THERE IS A BEAR IN YOUR OVEN?

A: THE OVEN DOOR WON'T CLOSE.

Finish the scene. Where is the bear in there?

Q: WHY WAS A PIG ON THE AIRPLANE?

A: BECAUSE ITS OWNER WANTED TO SEE PIGS FLY.

It's a pig! It's a plane! Fill the seats
with all sorts of characters!

Q: WHY DID THE TREE NEED
   TO TAKE A NAP?

A: BECAUSE IT WAS BUSHED!

Doodle a sleepy tree stretched out in the
flower bed, using the bush for a pillow.

Q: WHAT'S A BEE'S MOTTO?

A: "MIND YOUR OWN BEESWAX!"

What's in the hive? Bee busy and draw it!

Q: WHAT'S A BIRD'S MOTTO?

A: "THE EARLY BIRD GETS THE WORM!"

Fill in the balloon with her motto. Finish
the bird. Where's the worm?

Q: WHAT'S AN OTTER'S MOTTO?

A: "DO UNTO OTTERS AS YOU WOULD
HAVE THEM DO UNTO YOU!"

Where's her otter box? What's she playing
with? Finish the otter in the water.

Q: WHY DID THE BUNNY WORK AT THE HOTEL?

A: BECAUSE HE MADE A GOOD BELLHOP.

Whose bags is he carrying? Decorate the hotel lobby.

Q: WHAT DOES A HEN DO WHEN SHE PUTS HER CHRISTMAS SHOPPING LIST TOGETHER?

A: SHE MAKES A LIST AND CHICKS IT TWICE.

Design a shopping center for chickens all around her.

Q: WHAT HAPPENS WHEN A CAT EATS A LEMON?

A: SHE BECOMES A SOURPUSS.

Doodle the rest of the cat and her
lemony puckering ways.

Q: WHAT'S A WHALE'S FAVORITE CANDY?

A: BLUBBER GUM.

Blow this picture up by drawing more sea life
enjoying the gum . . . and saltwater taffy.

Q: WHAT DO YOU GET WHEN YOU CROSS A COW WITH A RABBIT?

A: HARE IN YOUR MILK.

Finish this crazy combination and
doodle the udderly hoppy joke.

Q: WHAT KIND OF ANIMAL WEARS
SHOES WHILE IT'S SLEEPING?

_____
A: A HORSE!

Doodle a horse-a-pedic bed around it.
What about barn windows behind it?

Q: WHY DID THE BUG GET UP EARLY EVERY MORNING?

A: BECAUSE IT WAS A PRAYING MANTIS.

Finish the drawing. What is the bug's prayer? Is it kneeling next to its bed?

What's on the moooon?

Q: WHY WOULDN'T THE PRINCESS TALK ABOUT WHO SHE KISSED?

A: SHE HAD A FROG IN HER THROAT.

Draw a toadily warty prince.

Q: WHAT'S THE BEST WAY TO PLAY A SCARY VIDEO GAME?

A: ON A BIG-SCREAM TV.

What's on the screaming big screen?

Q: WHAT KIND OF FRUIT SERVES FOOD?

A: A WAITER-MELON.

What food can you doodle? What's on the table?

Q: WHAT DO YOU CALL A TORO IN A TUTU?

A: A BULL-ERINA.

Doodle a dancing matador with an amazing cape.

Q: WHAT IS THE FASTEST RIDE FOR BREAD?

A: THE ROLLER-TOASTER.

Amuse us with a ride hidden in the hills.

Q: WHAT KIND OF BREAKFAST FOOD
WOULD YOU HAVE TO WIND UP?

A: A FLAPJACK-IN-A-BOX.

Doodle a pancake . . . and make it fun!

A: IT WAS ALWAYS TIED.

Who is the string racing? Glue? Scissors?

Q: WHAT DO YOU CALL A COW THAT CAN'T GIVE MILK?

A: A MILK DUD.

Where is the dairy farmer? Is he sad?
Where are the chickens?

KNOCK KNOCK.
   WHO'S THERE?
WEIRDO.
   WEIRDO WHO?
WEIRDO YOU THINK YOU'RE GOING?

Doodle a door and a frightened friend behind it.

Q: WHAT DO YOU GIVE A MOUSE ON HIS BIRTHDAY?

A: CHEESECAKE.

Doodle the rest of the cake with candles. Finish
the table and draw friends and balloons.

KNOCK KNOCK.
   WHO'S THERE?
RADIO.
   RADIO WHO?
RADIO OR NOT, HERE I COME!

Doodle a television answering the
door. Where is the remote?

Q: WHAT DID THE PEN SAY
TO THE PENCIL?

A: "YOU'RE LOOKING SHARP TODAY!"

Pick up a pencil and draw a pen.
What's the pencil's reply?

Q: WHAT DID THE MOTHER POSSUM
   SAY TO HER SON?

A: "QUIT HANGING AROUND ALL DAY
      AND DO SOMETHING!"

Doodle her son. What's below them?

KNOCK KNOCK.
  WHO'S THERE?
CONNOR.
  CONNOR WHO?
CONNOR BROTHER COME OUT TO PLAY?

Who's the knocker?

KNOCK KNOCK.
   WHO'S THERE?
CARRIE.
   CARRIE WHO?
CARRIE MY BOOKS FOR ME?

Finish the book-carrying character. Doodle
the door and the dude being asked.

Q: WHAT DO YOU CALL A FISH
   WITH NO EYES?

A: FSH.

Doodle the rest of the fish with no eyes.
Where is its seeing-eye dogfish?

Q: WHAT DID THE TREE SAY
   TO THE FLOWER?

A: "I'M ROOTING FOR YOU!"

Doodle a big, beautiful tree talking to its bud.

Q: WHAT DOES A SNOWMAN EAT FOR BREAKFAST?

A: FROSTED FLAKES.

Finish the munching snowman. What's in the bowl? What's on the box?

FREDA: TODAY THE TEACHER WAS
    YELLING AT ME FOR SOMETHING
    I DIDN'T DO!
MOM: WHAT WAS THAT?
FREDA: MY HOMEWORK.

Doodle Mom looking surprised.

Q: WHAT KIND OF DOG CRIES
   THE MOST?

A: CHI-WAH-WAH!

Finish the bawling little dog and draw its pal.

Q: WHAT DID THE TOMATO SAY TO THE MUSHROOM?

A: "YOU LOOK LIKE A FUNGI."

There's mush room on this page to doodle. Lettuce see you do it.

Q: WHAT DO YOU GET WHEN YOU CROSS A PIG WITH A CHRISTMAS TREE?

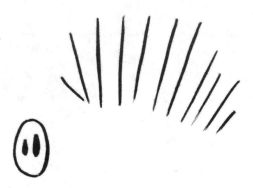

A: A PORK-U-PINE.

Finish this wacky combo and decorate it.

Q: NAME TWO DAYS OF THE WEEK THAT START WITH T.

A: "TODAY" AND "TOMORROW."

Fill in a funny calendar. Make up some crazy days.

A: A STICK-IN-THE-MUD.

Doodle the stick that is stuck. What's its friend saying?

Q: WHAT ARE THE FUNNIEST FISH AT THE AQUARIUM?

A: CLOWN FISH.

Finish the funny fish. Is there a clown school of fish?

Q: WHAT HAPPENS IF YOU PUT YOUR HEAD INSIDE A HOT AIR BALLOON BASKET?

A: YOU GET A FACE LIFT!

Who's in the basket? Add bright and beautiful designs to the balloon.

Q: WHERE DOES A LIZARD KEEP HIS GROCERIES?

A: IN THE REFRIGER-GATOR.

Doodle a lizard with a stack of cool items.

Q: WHAT DID THE OLD MAID LIVE IN?

A: A HOUSE OF CARDS.

Doodle a deck of cards made into her house.

Q: WHY DID THE CREDIT CARD
   GO TO JAIL?

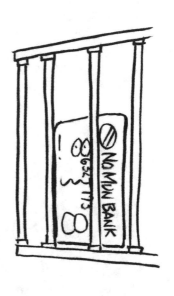

A: IT WAS GUILTY AS CHARGED!

Who's visiting? Cash? Check? Money order?

Q: WHAT DO YOU HAVE IF YOUR DOG CAN'T BARK?

A: A HUSHPUPPY.

Doodle a doggy who can't make a sound.
Where is its loudly dressed owner?

Q: WHY CAN'T YOU TRUST A PIG?

A: IT WILL ALWAYS SQUEAL ON YOU.

Give the pig some expression.

Q: WHAT FRUIT TEASES PEOPLE A LOT?

A: A BA-NA-NA-NA-NA-NA-NA!

Doodle the fruit being teased. Bad banana!

Q: WHAT KIND OF ANIMAL CONTRADICTS ITSELF?

A: A HIPPO-CRITE.

Finish hippo. What's it doing in the water?

Q: WHAT CANDY IS NEVER ON TIME?

A: CHOCO-LATE.

Where is the candy going? To a confection convention? Suh-weeeet!

A: "LET'S STICK TOGETHER!"

Where's the other one? Stick to the
task and doodle the scene!

Q: WHAT DID THE ALIEN SAY TO THE FLOWER BED?

A: "TAKE ME TO YOUR WEEDER."

Doodle an out-of-this-world alien with strange antennas and hands for feet.

Q: HOW COME HYENAS ARE SO
HEALTHY?

A: BECAUSE LAUGHTER IS THE BEST MEDICINE.

Finish hyena and draw a treadmill under it.

Q: WHAT GETS WET WHILE IT DRIES?

A: A TOWEL.

What used the towel? Your face? Your dog? Your cat?

Q: HOW DO SKUNKS GET IN TOUCH WITH EACH OTHER?

A: THEY USE THEIR SMELL PHONES.

To whom is the skunk sending this smellfie?

Q: WHAT IS AS BIG AS AN ELEPHANT BUT WEIGHS ZERO POUNDS?

A: THE ELEPHANT'S SHADOW.

Doodle the elephant's shadow. Any other shadowy creatures around?

Q: WHAT DID THE ELEVATOR SAY TO ITS FRIEND?

A: "I THINK I'M COMING DOWN WITH SOMETHING."

Who—or what—is the friend? Stairs?
Step? Spiral staircase? Rope?

Q: WHAT DOES A SQUIRREL LIKE TO EAT FOR BREAKFAST?

A: DOUGH-NUTS.

Finish squirrel. Don't forget his bushy
tail (with doughnuts hidden in it).

Q: WHY WAS EVERYONE LOOKING UP AT THE CEILING AND CHEERING?

A: THEY WERE CEILING FANS.

Doodle a decorative fan and add a person
(or animal) cheering between these two.

Q: WHAT DO BIRDS DO BEFORE THEY WORK OUT?

A: THEIR WORM-UPS.

Use your bird brain and finish the bird's head,
and don't forget her target . . . the worms.

Q: WHAT HAPPENS WHEN YOU PHONE A CLOWN THREE TIMES?

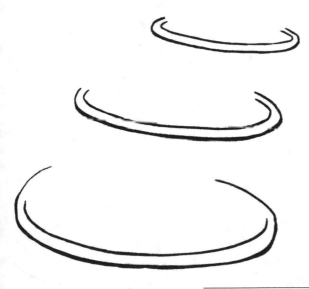

A: A THREE-RING CIRCUS.

Fill the three rings with circus performers.

CUSTOMER: EXCUSE ME, WAITER, BUT IS THERE SPAGHETTI ON THE MENU?
WAITER: NO, BUT I BELIEVE WE HAVE SOME IN THE KITCHEN.

Use your noodle and doodle the spaghetti. What else is in it?

Q: WHAT DO TREES EAT FOR BREAKFAST?

A: OAK-MEAL.

Doodle the top of the tree and what it's eating.

KNOCK, KNOCK.
   WHO'S THERE?
PAWS.
   PAWS WHO?
CAN YOU PAWS FOR A MINUTE AND
   OPEN THE DOOR?

Whose two paws are these? Finish
doodling the door too!

Draw yourself on the building—enlarged—telling
your favorite big-city joke. Add some city buildings
and some joke listeners . . . anyone you know?

Q: WHERE DID THE CAT BUY A FOAM HAND FOR THE CHAMPIONSHIP GAME?

A: AT THE PAW-N SHOP.

Finish the cat's head. Is she wearing the team hat?

A: THEY KNOW A LITTLE ABOUT GETTING DOWN.

Doodle ducks holding the bar. Who else is in line?

KNOCK KNOCK.
   WHO'S THERE?
EUNICE.
   EUNICE WHO?
EUNICE CYCLE.

Draw Eunice.

Doodle yourself telling a great barnyard joke. Add a horse and pig . . . and make them a laughing stock.

Q: WHY DIDN'T THE ROBIN USE THE BIRDBATH?

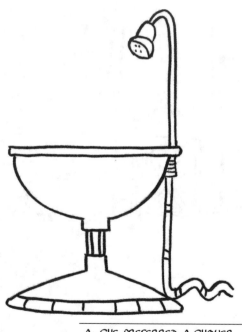

A: SHE PREFERRED A SHOWER.

Doodle a robin taking a shower, scrubbing her feathers, and bubbling with soap.

Q: WHAT HAPPENS WHEN A PORCUPINE BECOMES FRIENDS WITH A CACTUS?

A: THEY STICK TOGETHER.

Doodle other friends who are stuck too, right next to porcupine.

Write your dad's favorite joke. And doodle it too!

Q: HOW CAN YOU TELL A PIÑATA IS EXCITED?

A: SHE CAN'T CONTAIN HERSELF.

Who hit the donkey? Draw other candy
and toys flying out. Other kids too!

Write your mom's favorite joke. Doodle it too!

Q: WHAT HAPPENED WITH THE GIRL WHO THOUGHT SHE WASHED THE DISHES?

A: SHE DISH-COVERED THEY WERE STILL DIRTY!

Come clean and doodle a pile of dirty dishes.

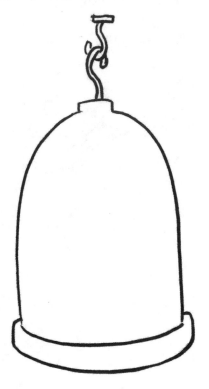

A: CANARY UNDERWOOD.

Doodle the harmonious little feathery
friend who can really warble.

Q: WHAT IS A CHICKEN'S FAVORITE COMPOSER?

A: BACH, BACH, BACH!

Doodle a barnyard full of animals
and their instruments.

Q: WHY DID THE HORSE BREAK INTO A TROT?

A: SHE GOT ASKED TO THE BARN DANCE.

Doodle other barnyard animals dancing too!

Q: WHAT DID THE GROOM SPIDER SAY TO HIS BRIDE?

A: "WITH THIS STRING, I DO THEE WEB."

Doodle a delicate doily-like web for the creepy couple.

Q: WHY DON'T BUNNIES TELL SCARY STORIES?

A: BECAUSE IT MAKES THE HARE STAND UP ON THE BACK OF THEIR NECKS.

Doodle other scared bunnies around a campfire.

KNOCK KNOCK.
  WHO'S THERE?
SARAH.
  SARAH WHO?
SARAH DOCTOR IN THE HOUSE? I'M
  SICK!

Doodle a doctor at the door.

Q: WHAT IS A SNOWMAN'S HEAVENLY GUARDIAN?

A: A SNOW ANGEL.

Draw the celestial impression in
the snow. Who made it?

Q: WHERE ARE SHEEP FROM?

A: THE BAA-HAMAS.

Fill out the scene and the surroundings. Add sheep.

Q: WHAT WAS INSIDE THE COOKIE'S COMPUTER?

A: CHOCOLATE CHIPS.

What would that look like?

A: IN A NURSERY!

Doodle a nursery and a caretaker for it.

Q: WHAT DO YOU CALL A SPORTS TEAM
ENTHUSIAST ON A STOOL?

A: A CHAIR LEADER!

Rah-rah-doodle! Gimme a megaphone in the
left hand and pom-poms in the right!

A: CLARINET.

Doodle the joke and notes flying everywhere.

Q: WHAT IS THE FASTEST PEANUT
   BUTTER IN THE WORLD?

A: JIFFY.

Bubble letter the name on the jar.
Who is P. B. jammin' with?

Q: WHAT DID ONE CANDLE SAY TO ANOTHER?

A: "DO YOU WANT TO GO OUT TONIGHT?"

Doodle his date melting from his warmth.

Q: WHAT'S A CHEF'S FAVORITE KIND OF PLANT?

Doodle a happy chef with pan and spatula.

Q: WHAT DO YOU CALL A COUPLE
   LITTLE TYKES ON A SEESAW?

A: TEETER-TODDLERS.

Doodle the other toddler . . . and background toys.

KNOCK KNOCK.
   WHO'S THERE?
LEAH.
   LEAH WHO?
LEAH THE DOOR UNLOCKED NEXT TIME!

Finish the scene.

Q: WHAT SHOW DID THE GIRL ON THE BEACH WANT TO BE ON?

A: DANCING WITH THE STARFISH.

Doodle a dancing starfish. Where are the fishy judges?

A: SHE WAS GROUNDED.

Doodle a leaping little lady . . . is it you?

Q: WHEN DOES YOUR DINNER NEVER GET HOT?

A: WHEN IT'S CHILI.

What in the world is in this chili? Doodle it!

KNOCK KNOCK.
  WHO'S THERE?
AMANDA.
  AMANDA WHO?
AMANDA FIX THE PLUMBING IS AT THE
  DOOR.

Doodle the joke.

Q: WHEN IS A VOLLEYBALL REALLY SHARP?

A: WHEN IT'S SPIKED.

Doodle a spiked volleyball. Who is
hitting it from the other side?

Q: WHAT IS A LIGHTNING BUG'S FAVORITE GAME?

A: HIDE-AND-GLOW-SEEK.

Would it bug you to doodle the joke?

KNOCK KNOCK.
   WHO'S THERE?
DAWN.
   DAWN WHO?
DAWN MESS AROUND OR I'M LEAVING!

Doodle a door and who is behind it.

KNOCK KNOCK.
  WHO'S THERE?
EILEEN.
  EILEEN WHO?
EILEEN DOVER AND FELL OFF THE
  PORCH.

Doodle who answered the door and her surprised look.

KNOCK KNOCK.
  WHO'S THERE?
MIA.
  MIA WHO?
MIA HAND IS KILLING ME FROM ALL
  THIS KNOCKING. WILL YOU PLEASE
  LET ME IN?

Doodle a door . . . and a window on
the door with a face in it.

A: HAND-ME-DOWNS.

Doodle the joke.

Q: WHAT DID THE FLOWER SAY TO
THE FLOWER HOLDER?

A: "LET'S PUT A SMILE ON YOUR VASE!"

Give it a smile and fill the holder
with awesome flowers!

Q: WHAT DOES A GIRL DO IN HISTORY CLASS?

A: SHE REWRITES HIS-TORY AND MAKES IT HER-STORY.

Doodle a girl writing at her desk.

A: SHE WANTED A SLEEPING BAG.

Doodle a lullaby-singing lady.

Q: WHY IS A DOG ATTRACTED
   TO THE TEAKETTLE?

A: BECAUSE IT WHISTLES.

Doodle a design on the kettle.
Where is the excited doggy?

KNOCK KNOCK.
   WHO'S THERE?
FRIEDA.
   FRIEDA WHO?
FRIEDA ANIMALS, I WANT TO PLAY WITH
   THEM!

What's in the cage? Who's at the door?

A: PLASTIC SURGERY.

Doodle a dog with a tummy ache.

Q: HOW DO YOU WASH YOUR LITTLE FURRY DOG?

A: WITH YOUR SHAMPOODLE.

Doodle the poodle. Who's washing the dog?
Finish the tub, and make some more bubbles!

A: LITTLE RED RIDING HOODIE.

Where's the wolf?

Q: WHICH KIND OF KIDS DO TIGERS LIKE BEST?

A: GRRRRLS!

Finish tiger! Make him paws-itively
purrr-fect! Where's the grrrl?

Q: WHAT SCHOOL DANCE DID THE GEOMETRY TEACHER HOST?

A: A SQUARE DANCE.

Doodle square's partner. Is it a triangle
or circle? Do they have faces?

Q: WHAT IS A CLOWN'S FAVORITE ITALIAN DISH?

A: BOWTIE PASTA.

Doodle it! And the rest of this silly scene.

A: A MAKEUP PARTY!

Finish the face all made up.

KNOCK KNOCK.
  WHO'S THERE?
FRANCE.
  FRANCE WHO?
FRANCE STICK CLOSER THAN A
  BROTHER.

Doodle the door and the friend who is answering it.

Q: WHAT IS THE HOPPIEST EXERCISE TOY?

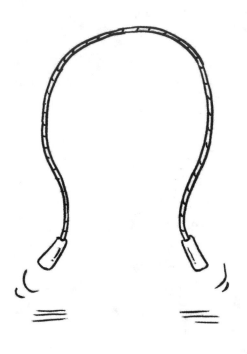

A: A JUMPY ROPE.

Who's doing the jumping?

Q: WHAT HAPPENED TO THE
   SNOW-WOMEN'S FRIENDSHIP
   AFTER THE BLIZZARD?

A: IT DRIFTED.

Doodle a drift and bring life to these
cool ladies of the snow.

Q: WHY DID THE GROWING GIRL FEEL
   SO AWKWARD?

A: SHE GREW ANOTHER FOOT.

Doodle the rest of her.

A: HER BREATH.

Finish her handle and net and the butterflies she caught and will catch.

Q: WHY DID THE CHEF HAVE TO STOP COOKING?

A: SHE RAN OUT OF THYME!

What's on the chef's spice rack? What about herbs?

Q: WHAT IS A BABY'S FAVORITE PASTA DISH?

A: GOO-GOO-LASH.

Finish the scene. Fill up the plate with pasta.

Q: HOW DO YOU UNDERSTAND A BIRD CALL?

A: WITH AN IN-CHIRP-RETER.

Doodle you with binoculars. What is the bird saying?

A: MICE CUBES.

Doodle the cat who's going to lap this up.

Q: WHERE DOES A SUPERHERO VACATION?

A: ANYWHERE THAT STARTS WITH "THE CAPE."

Finish this superhero and write your own
super joke beneath it. Starring you?

Q: WHY WAS THE SEWING MACHINE
   SO FUNNY?

A: IT KEPT EVERYONE IN STITCHES!

Who is sewing? Sew what? What is being sewn?

Q: WHY DID CINDERELLA GET KICKED
   OUT OF THE SOCCER GAME?

A: SHE RAN AWAY FROM THE BALL.

Doodle Cinderella's hair and legs and slippers!

Q: WHY DID THE GIRL NEED A LADDER TO GO TO SCHOOL?

A: BECAUSE IT WAS HIGH SCHOOL.

Where is she climbing? Who is there with her?

About the Author

Rob Elliott is the author of *Laugh-Out-Loud Jokes for Kids, More Laugh-Out-Loud Jokes for Kids, Laugh-Out-Loud Animal Jokes for Kids,* and *Knock-Knock Jokes for Kids* and has been a publishing professional for more than twenty years. Rob lives in **West Michigan,** where in his spare time he enjoys laughing out loud with his wife and five children.

About the Illustrator

Jonny Hawkins is a full-time cartoonist whose work has appeared in over six hundred publications, including *Reader's Digest*, *Parade Magazine*, *The Saturday Evening Post*, and *Guideposts*. His illustrations have appeared in many books including the Chicken Soup for the Soul series, and he has created forty-eight successful page-a-day cartoon calendars (over four hundred thousand sold). He works from his home in **Sherwood, Michigan**, where he lives with his wife, Carissa, and their three children, four cats, and a dog.

Need More Laughs?

- - - - - - - - * - - - - - - - -

Visit

LOLJokesForKids.com

to submit your own joke,
receive FREE printable doodle pages,
and watch the video!

• • •

Doodles for
Everyone!

 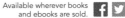